CATECHESIS WITH THE SPIRIT

CATECHESIS WITH THE SPIRIT

THE TEN PATHS OF CATECHETICAL SPIRITUALITY

CARDINAL VÍCTOR MANUEL FERNÁNDEZ

Paulist Press
New York / Mahwah, NJ

Cover image by Ridderhof/Pixabay.com
Cover design by Joe Gallagher
Book design by Lynn Else

Originally published in Spanish as *Catequesis con Espíritu* by Agape Libros, Av. San Martín 6863, (1419) Autonomous City of Buenos Aires - Argentina
www.agape-libros.com.ar

Library of Congress Cataloging-in-Publication Data
Names: Fernández, Victor M. (Victor Manuel), 1962– author.
Title: Catechesis with the Spirit: the ten paths of catechetical spirituality / Cardinal Victor Manuel Fernández.
Other titles: Catequesis con Espíritu. English
Description: New York : Paulist Press, [2025] | "Originally published in Spanish as Catequesis con Espíritu by Agape Libros, Av. San Martín 6863, (1419)"—Title page verso. | Includes bibliographical references. | Summary: "This book outlines ten main features that cultivate a specific catechetical spiritual culture in a parish"—Provided by publisher.
Identifiers: LCCN 2024010250 (print) | LCCN 2024010251 (ebook) | ISBN 9780809157211 (paperback) | ISBN 9780809188840 (e-book)
Subjects: LCSH: Catechists—Religious life. | Catechetics—Catholic Church.
Classification: LCC BX1968 .F4713 2025 (print) | LCC BX1968 (ebook) | DDC 268/.82—dc23/eng/20241001
LC record available at https://lccn.loc.gov/2024010250
LC ebook record available at https://lccn.loc.gov/2024010251

ISBN 978-0-8091-5721-1 (paperback)
ISBN 978-0-8091-8884-0 (ebook)

Published by Paulist Press
997 Macarthur Boulevard
Mahwah, New Jersey 07430
www.paulistpress.com

Printed and bound in the
United States of America

CONTENTS

ACRONYMS

AG	*Ad gentes* (Second Vatican Council)
AL	*Amoris laetitia* (Francis)
CT	*Catechesi tradendae* (Saint John Paul II)
EG	*Evangelii gaudium* (Francis)
EN	*Evangelii nuntiandi* (Saint Paul VI)
GS	*Gaudium et spes* (Second Vatican Council)
NMI	*Novo millennio ineunte* (Saint John Paul II)
PO	*Presbyterorum ordinis* (Second Vatican Council)
RMi	*Redemptoris missio* (Saint John Paul II)
SD	*Documento de Santo Domingo*
ST	*Summa theologica* (Saint Thomas Aquinas)

INTRODUCTION

The Spirituality of the Catechist

When it comes to the spirituality of the catechist, unfortunately it is often said that it is the same as that of a priest, a nun, or a monk. For example, it is said that the spirituality of the catechist is made up of personal prayer, reading the Bible, and the Eucharist, and the Liturgy of the Hours is often added. But then one is not speaking of a specific spirituality of the catechist, or even of a spirituality, but only of some means of spirituality common to all Christians.

The spirituality that characterizes a catechist, like any other Christian spirituality, is *marked by the notes of its mission*. These are not spaces of spirituality lived apart from that mission, as if one were taking an intimate parenthesis to dedicate oneself to God and as if the catechetical task were not "spiritual."[1]

One's own mission is not an appendix or a part of one's own existence. The mission deeply marks life and identity in such a way that one understands oneself as transformed by that mission. The name "Jesus," which means "God saves," indicates that Jesus was completely marked by his mission as Savior. The same should happen with a catechist soul. A good catechist identifies so much with their mission that they could add it to their name: "Martha Catechist García," "Francis Catechist Braun."

In this way, we understand that spirituality must also be marked by the catechetical mission. The catechist is called to live a spiritual depth in his or her own mission. If this is the case, when the catechist has a moment of contemplation in prayer, what he or she contemplates remains in his or her heart when he or she goes to give catechesis, and he or she lives it in the catechetical activity itself.

Furthermore, what is contemplated in prayer becomes more mature when it goes into action and is communicated to others. In communication, what one has contemplated is enriched, expressed, applied, and deepened, and it projects and grows in the exercise of the catechetical ministry.

As a consequence, when the catechist finishes a catechetical encounter and returns for a moment of recollection, that solitary engagement with God will be richer than the previous one, because now he will be loaded with the richness that life has given him, and more specifically, with what he experienced at the catechesis meeting.

Spirituality is the dynamism of love that the Spirit instills in our hearts and permeates our entire life. But that dynamism of love is marked, enriched, adorned, and embellished by distinctive characteristics that come from the mission that one must carry out, from the specific task that one must perform for others.

Therefore, a catechist does not love in the same way that a monk or an itinerant preacher does. They love in a different way, with a different style, with a different passion.

We can say that when a task is lived in an appropriate way, a *spiritual culture* is created that is proper to that *mission* received from God. This spiritual culture is transmitted each time a new catechist joins a community of catechists, and spontaneously acquires—as if by osmosis—the characteristics of the spirituality of their mission. But this only happens if there is truly a "catechetical spiritual culture" in that community of catechists. That is to say, if the specific spirituality of catechetical action has truly been incarnated in that community; if that specific spirituality has become a kind of "community treasure" that gives life and dynamism. In that case, Christian spirituality has truly been "incarnated" in the catechetical mission.

Evangelizing spirituality is a path of communal sanctification in the exercise of the apostolic mission. This path does not leave out any part of evangelizing activity. Everything must be placed under the impulse of the Spirit of holiness. Everything must be raised up in the presence of the Holy God, imploring together his light, his help, and his forgiveness. Therefore, the responsible and participatory path of pastoral planning, execution, and evaluation in the light of the Word also forms part of this process of communal sanctification. We need to overcome all forms of dualism, as if organization were a different or separate reality from life according to the Spirit.

When the moment of catechesis arrives, after having prepared it throughout the week, it will be a spiritual and pastoral act at the same time. The words and the encounter with others will then be charged with a deep meaning, and thus the encounter nourishes, sanctifies, and fulfills the catechist.

Not only is the moment of prayer spiritual, but the entire preparation has also been made with love, which gives meaning, joy, clarity, and security to the catechist in the catechetical encounter and can lead to a true mystical experience in the midst of that encounter with others.

This pastoral activity thus becomes deeply satisfying, and instead of wearing out the catechist, it fills them with life. Thus, the moment of rest after the encounter will not be the unplugging of an empty and jaded heart, the equivalent of a weight being lifted off one's shoulders, but the repose of a deeply satisfied heart.

The encounter with others should not be an obstacle that limits our contemplative possibilities. To affirm this would be to reestablish a marked dualism between intimacy and exteriority, between subjectivity and action, between solitude and encounter with the other, understanding exteriority, action, and encounter with others as enemies of contemplation.

Let us see together how this specific modality of being spiritual is lived in the catechetical mission by studying the ten basic characteristics of the spirituality of catechesis, that is, the mysticism proper to catechetical activity.

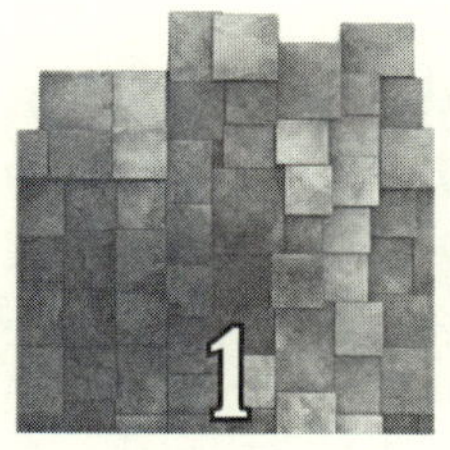

IN LOVE WITH JESUS THE TEACHER

First of all, let me say that the very image of Jesus that a catechist has is marked by his or her catechetical mission. The Jesus that he or she contemplates in his or her prayer and meditation is the Jesus teacher, the Jesus catechist. He is the Jesus who distributes the bread of his Word and sows his life in the hearts of people. He is the one who stopped to catechize the Samaritan woman, Zacchaeus, and the sinners. The catechist is so identified and imbued with the mission that he or she receives from Jesus that he or she cannot help but look at Jesus as a catechist.

Therefore, when the catechist contemplates Jesus in prayer, when he or she adores him and dialogues with him, in that same prayer he or she feels impelled to be a catechist like Jesus. Right there, in private prayer, the desire for the catechetical encounter should spring forth.

It is not that he or she goes to prayer to draw strength to be able to "endure" a catechetical encounter. He or she does not go to prayer to rest in the Lord after having exerted himself or herself greatly in catechesis. If that were the case, his or her spiritual life would be on the margins of his or her mission. For the true catechist, in the same personal prayer, the desire (like a fire that cannot be extinguished) to begin the catechetical encounter springs forth. At the end of the encounter, he or she returns to meet with the divine Master to thank him happily that he or she has been able to be his instrument to reach others with his Word.

Let us look at Jesus: he was not a mystic isolated from the people and the world; rather, he lived his spirituality completely immersed in history and in relationship with others. He went back and forth along the roads of Galilee without ceasing to contemplate the birds and the flowers of his land, and he invited his disciples to pay attention, to contemplate things and life, to perceive the message of nature (Luke 12:24, 27; John 4:35). He ate and drank with sinners (Matt 11:19), and he enjoyed spending time with the children of his town (Mark 10:13–16). He could stop to converse with the Samaritan woman (John 4:27) or with Nicodemus (John 3:1–3). He allowed himself to have his feet washed by prostitutes (Luke 7:36–50), and he stopped to touch the sick with his own saliva (Mark 7:33). When he spoke to someone, he did not endure it reluctantly but rather fixed his gaze with a deep loving attention: "Jesus [looked] at him [and] loved him" (Mark 10:21).

He was attentive to the smallest gestures of kindness of his people and was capable of marveling at the poor: "He also saw a poor widow put in two small copper coins" (Luke 21:2).

That empathy with his land and his people certainly

characterized Jesus's way of loving, and was therefore part of his "everyday" spirituality:

> For the very Word made flesh willed to share in the human fellowship. He was present at the wedding of Cana, visited the house of Zacchaeus, ate with publicans and sinners. He revealed the love of the Father and the sublime vocation of man in terms of the most common of social realities and by making use of the speech and the imagery of plain everyday life. Willingly obeying the laws of his country He sanctified those human ties, especially family ones, which are the source of social structures. He chose to lead the life proper to an artisan of His time and place. (GS 32)

Jesus was certainly not a person separated from the poor and simple, nor did he consider them uneducated, ignorant, imperfect, or unworthy of his treatment. His relationship with the people aroused affection and admiration. It was rather the powerful—and some small groups reduced to serving them—who persecuted Jesus and orchestrated his arrest while the people in general identified with him. This is evidenced by John 7:45–49, where the authorities are seen trying to arrest Jesus, while the simple people listened to him in admiration. The conclusion of the elitist authorities confirms the reality: "Has any one of the authorities or of the Pharisees believed in him? But this crowd, which does not know the law—they are accursed" (7:48–49).

Nor were the Apostles elitist beings, secluded in small groups of the select, isolated from the life of their people. The Book of Acts insists on emphasizing that, while the authorities harassed them, they enjoyed the sympathy of all the people (Acts 2:47; 4:21, 33; 5:13).

Following the model of Jesus, every catechist is called to immerse himself or herself fully in the land where he or she lives with "the same motive which led Christ to bind Himself, in virtue of His Incarnation, to certain social and cultural conditions of those human beings among whom He dwelt" (AG 10), and he or she must reflect his or her spirituality "in the social and cultural framework of their own homeland, according to their own national traditions" (AG 21).

In this way, "through direct experience" (RM 53), catechists are "familiar with their national and religious traditions; let them gladly and reverently lay bare the seeds of the Word which lie hidden among their fellows." Thus they can experience the joy of learning "by sincere and patient dialogue what treasures a generous God has distributed among the nations of the earth" (AG 11). This is a spirituality that is worldly, but sacredly worldly, because it is capable of contemplating the signs of God in the world and in the life of its people.

Only in this way will catechists be able to transmit the gospel "in a credible and fruitful way" in a place. Only then will they be " understanding, appreciating, fostering and evangelizing" the environment in which they work (RM 53).

For all this, the catechist cannot think that his or her spirituality is merely the moments of solitude, when he or she can be in silence with Jesus and free himself or herself from the world and from others. On the contrary, when he or she meets Jesus in solitude, he or she feels a pressing call to share the life of the people—like

Jesus—to love and serve. His or her spirituality is a way of loving, it is the depth with which he or she looks at and listens to others, it is his or her ability to discover the action of the Spirit in others, it is a contemplative gaze in the midst of life, like that of Mary, who "treasured all these things in her heart" (Luke 2:51).

Above all, the great spiritual moment will be the catechetical encounter, where all his or her capacity to love, to contemplate the Word, to give himself or herself to others, to enjoy the presence of Jesus, to perceive the signs of grace will be concentrated. Certainly, although the moments of prayerful solitude are indispensable, the best nourishment for his or her spirituality will be a well-lived catechetical encounter: lived in the presence of the Lord, with love and for love. Above all, there he or she will find Jesus, his or her Master, and there he or she will be an instrument of the grace that will sanctify him or her.

Personal Journey

For your personal growth in catechetical spirituality, I propose three tasks:

a. At some moments of prayer, dedicate yourself to slowly going through the narratives of the Gospels, in the presence of Jesus, to contemplate in the texts the different attitudes of Jesus as a catechist.
b. Jesus has a particular gaze for each person. It is a gaze always full of love, understanding, and encouragement, but it is not the same for everyone, because it adapts

to what each one needs according to their temperament and what they are living. I propose that you remember in prayer, one by one, all your catechumens, and imagine how Jesus would look at each one of them.

c. Imagine how the next catechetical encounter would be if you lived it with deep spirituality, if you did everything only for love, without expecting recognition. If you lived it discovering Jesus in the midst of the group, looking at each one with tenderness. And when the next meeting comes, try to live it in that more spiritual way.

THOSE FEW FACES

Even when the catechist withdraws into solitude to have a personal encounter with Jesus, others cannot be absent. For if he has taken his mission seriously, he will never be able to remove them from his heart when he approaches Jesus in solitude.

That is why intercession occupies a very special place and power in the catechist's personal prayer and in his encounter with the Eucharist. It is true for all Christians; but in the intercession of the catechist, a few faces predominate: the faces of his catechumens, with their very concrete and personal stories.

In front of Jesus, the catechist recalls those few faces and what he has experienced with them in the catechetical encounter. He speaks with Jesus about what he has perceived in their looks, in their words, in their gestures. He prays to Jesus for that sadness he saw in John, for that nervousness that assails Julia, for that shyness that limits Eduardo. In this way, his prayer is also a profound act of love for neighbor.

Many times we have the wrong idea about what a contemplative or spiritual person is. We believe that someone is more spiritual when he thinks only of God and is not distracted by memories, thoughts about people, or human affections. This is a tremendous error that has nothing to do with a healthy spirituality, because how can he "who do[es] not love a brother or sister whom they have seen...love [a] God whom they have not seen"? (1 John 4:20). Let us see an example.

Certainly, Saint Paul was very spiritual. However, let us observe what was the content of his prayer:

> We always give thanks to God for all of you
> and mention you in our prayers, constantly.
> (1 Thess 1:2–3)

> [I] constantly pray...with joy in every one of
> my prayers for all of you. (Phil 1:4)

When Saint Paul prayed, he was constantly remembering his spiritual children, and in all his prayers he prayed for them. This means that our spirituality has to incorporate others, particularly those whom God has entrusted to us.

This ability to concentrate his love on a few people to whom he has been sent makes the catechist a shepherd, a father, and a mother for them. The catechist is also a "shepherd" of his catechumens, although in a different way than the priest. The priest is a shepherd by virtue of specific functions he cannot delegate, which are to celebrate the Eucharist and to impart sacramental absolution, that is, as an instrument of the gift of sanctifying grace, which is poured out especially in these sacraments. In this way he gives life to the sheep and heals them. But the catechist also does this from the ministry of the Word: he leads his catechumens to the green pastures and to the fountains of supernatural water that restores (Ps 23:2–3), and thus he heals them (Ezek 34:4, 16).

He brings them closer to the Eucharist, helps them to pray, teaches them to love with generosity, and thus gives them the water of life.

For this reason, the catechist exercises the function of father and mother toward his catechumens. The Second Vatican Council taught us that the whole community is a mother "through charity, prayer, example, and works of penance" (PO 6). But each one exercises this motherhood of the community in a more direct way with those who have been entrusted to him particularly. For this reason, the catechist is in a special way father and mother of his catechumens (1 Thess 2:7–8, 11–12); he begets for God and accompanies his spiritual children on their journey. Here is located the Marian dimension of catechesis, because from Mary we learn welcome, closeness, tenderness, delicacy, and maternal care.

And in terms of the closeness and intimate knowledge that the shepherd has of his sheep (John 10:14), the catechist is more of a shepherd and more of a father-mother than the priest because his treatment is certainly more frequent and closer. A sign of this is that, while the parish priest often does not know the names of all the children, young people, and adults who attend catechesis, the catechists know much more than their names. In this sense, they are a more diaphanous sign of God as a father who calls us by our own name.

But the spirituality of the catechist implies the deep conviction of being an instrument and reflection of Christ, who is the true and principal Shepherd. Above all in him they must find the firm and guiding love of a father and the tenderness of a mother. For this reason, the affection of the catechist is sincere and warm, but at the same time detached and oblative because he is primarily interested in the good of the catechumens and their encounter with Christ. That is why Jesus said to Peter: “Feed my sheep” (John 21:17). Catechesis does not exist in the first place so that the catechumens can become friends with the catechist and keep a good memory of him but so that, through him, they can find life, strength, and joy in the Lord. There is the deepest joy of the fruitfulness of the catechist.

His healthy pride will not be to say that the catechumens have never forgotten him, but that they live the gospel and let themselves be guided by the Spirit: “You yourselves are our letter, written on our hearts… not with ink but with the Spirit of the living God” (2 Cor 3:2–3).

Those few faces, close and particularly loved, are the permanent object of his gaze and his contemplative memory.

Personal Journey

a. Enter the presence of God and begin to remember the faces of your catechumens. Look at them with love and try to recognize in each face their sufferings, their tiredness, their wounds, their fears, their difficulties, and also their joys, their abilities, and their good feelings. Talk to Jesus about all of this, ask him for the deep needs of each of them, and thank him for the good things.

b. Offer yourself to the Lord as an instrument to reach each one of them with all your gestures and actions. Ask Jesus to take over your whole being so that it is he who acts in your catechesis. Closing your eyes, imagine your hands, and offer them to be instruments of caress, of closeness. Imagine your own face, and ask Jesus to transform it with his own expressions of love, strength, and compassion. Imagine your mouth, and offer it so that only the appropriate and necessary words come out of it. Imagine your whole body, and ask Jesus that through all your movements he himself may manifest to the catechumens.

REFLECTIONS ON A PLEASING WORD

Certainly, the Word of God occupies a central place in catechetical spirituality. But not only is that Word at the center of personal prayer, it is also the spiritual nucleus of the catechetical encounter. Above all, this is why the catechetical encounter is not a class; it is a community encounter with the Word. In transmitting the Word to the catechumens, the catechist is contemplating it, enjoying it, listening to it himself, and letting himself be touched. In the midst of the encounter, he is inwardly thanking for the gift of the Word, expressing his love for it, and experiencing it.

It is true that his relationship with the Word in the catechetical encounter will be richer and more joyful if he has previously contemplated it in solitary prayer, if he has ruminated on it serenely in his intimacy, if he has applied it to his own life in prolonged meditation.

If the gospel is a proposal for life and is ordered to produce a determined way of living, the first spiritual attitude of the catechist will be to welcome it into his own existence, to carry it to his own heart, to make it flesh within him. In this way, the catechetical encounter will consist of "communicating to others what has been contemplated" (ST II 188, 6).

It is a matter not only of leading a perfect moral life but also and above all (and as a condition of this) of having a personal relationship with God in his Word that is reflected in the way he speaks of it. A catechist who has been alone with the Word transmits it with strength, conviction, and passion, and that is contagious.

This has at the same time a great pastoral importance, since "modern man listens more willingly to witnesses than to teachers" (EN 41). Authenticity—which is so highly valued in the world today—"the world is calling for evangelizers to speak to it of a God whom the evangelists themselves should know and be familiar with as if they could see the invisible" (EN 76).

Consequently, it should be normal for the catechist to use for his personal meditation the same biblical text that he will have to transmit to his catechumens, and not another text. Using a text different from that of the catechetical encounter would lead him to develop a personal prayer parallel to his activity and without direct relation to it.

The catechist, if he acts moved by the dynamism of the Spirit, will be permanently oriented to the Word. He will avoid preaching himself or enclosing himself in a certain mental schema or in a few ideas that attract him. Not only will he respect and love the Word of God, but he will prostrate himself before it with a disposition of joyful submission, as a humble servant. From this attitude, he will be a permanent seeker of the profound meaning of that Word so that he can communicate it to others.[2]

It is worth pausing on this beautiful meditation by Pope Paul VI:

> The Gospel entrusted to us is also the word of truth. A truth which liberates and which alone gives peace of heart....The difficult truth that we seek in the Word of God and of which, we repeat, we are neither the masters nor the owners, but the depositaries, the heralds and the servants.
>
> Every evangelizer is expected to have a reverence for truth, especially since the truth that he studies and communicates is none other than revealed truth and hence, more than any other, a sharing in the first truth which is God Himself. The preacher of the Gospel will therefore be a person who even at the price of personal renunciation and suffering always seeks the truth that he must transmit to others. He never betrays or hides truth out of a desire to please men, in order to astonish or to shock, nor for the sake of originality or a desire to make an impression. He does not refuse truth. He does not obscure revealed truth by being too idle to search for it, or for the sake of his own comfort, or out of fear. He does not neglect to study it. He serves it generously, without making it serve him. (EN 78)

Therefore, it is a matter not only of praying with the Word but also of studying it, of trying to understand its real message. When I, as a catechist, dedicate myself to studying the Word of God that I am going to communicate, this study is at the same time a spiritual and pastoral attitude:

- It is spiritual because it is the expression of a "worship of truth" (EN 78), of a great love for the Word. Because I do not want to preach what I think but what that Word truly says, and I am afraid of mishandling it.
- It is pastoral because the catechetical activity is not to try to get others to connect with my ideas, with some striking resource, with my pedagogical skill. It is not to seek to have them say that I am an interesting person. It is not even to try to instill in them my own spirituality.

The catechetical activity in its deepest sense is to try to get others to meet Christ and grow in love, to produce an encounter with what Christ says in that concrete text.

It will be necessary to read the Word over and over again until it becomes clearer. It will also be necessary to read the notes, or some commentary. It will be necessary to consult with someone if there is something that seems obscure or complicated. It is not a matter of perfectly understanding all the details. This process of searching leads me to find the axis of the biblical text, its central message. But this study at the same time allows me to become familiar with the biblical text, to make it close and personal, so that I can speak to others about something that I have truly tried.

However, it is not enough to understand the message. We must allow that Word to speak to our own lives, to our concrete existence, so that I do not demand that others allow themselves to be existentially challenged by that Word if I have not first allowed myself to be "touched" by it.

By allowing that Word to be "incarnated" in our own lives, the catechist can be a true instrument of God who wants neither functionaries nor passive instruments. This path of personalization requires a conscious cooperation of the catechist in his encounter with the Word. In that prayerful encounter with a biblical text, he can help himself with some questions. For example: What does this text say to me, what does it motivate me to do? What does it ask of me? What bothers me, and why does it bother me? What am I trying to escape from and why? What do I like?

Through these questions it is possible to discover what God wants to say to you personally, in a loving dialogue made in the light of the Holy Spirit. For this, an interior silence is necessary, a receptive space that welcomes the light of Christ that is gloriously poured out.[3] A silence that allows the Word to touch one's own existence, to ask something of it, to transform it, to illuminate it.

But it is also true that the catechist's prayer with the Word should not be intimate or individualistic. When he is praying with the Word, the apostolic attitude should spring up right there. In the same personal prayer with the biblical text, the catechist begins to ask himself what God wants to say to his catechumens with that Word. Love for God always immediately becomes an impulse of love for neighbor, and therefore contemplation of God always tends to become an inclination toward neighbor. Thus, in his encounter with the Word, the catechist feels the impulse to incorporate the catechumens into his meditation with the Word.

This makes the catechist, in his relationship with the Word, very sincere, very open, very sensitive. Because when there is something in that Word that he does not understand, that does not tell him anything, that does not motivate him, instead of escaping from these difficulties by hiding in an abstraction or in an easy and quick explanation, the catechist reacts by thinking of his catechumens: "If this Word does not tell me anything, how am I going to motivate them to receive it sincerely?" "If I rebel against this Word, how will I help them to understand it and accept its message?" Then he begins to implore the help of grace and makes a new personal effort to let himself be spoken to by the Word, to let himself be touched and personally moved.

That Word, studied, contemplated, applied to one's own life, is the one that one will communicate with passion in the catechetical encounter. And others will be infected by perceiving that enthusiasm and that love.

The catechetical encounter itself thus becomes a contemplative moment of the Word. It is a matter not only of what St. Thomas Aquinas called "communicating what has been contemplated" but also of making the catechesis itself a profoundly spiritual act. In this way, a spiritual contemplation is realized in the very communication of the message. When the catechist is speaking to others about the Word, he is not just another professional but a lover who is loving each phrase he reads in the Word; he is savoring each thing he says about that beloved Word.

Personal Journey

I propose that you begin to practice the *Lectio divina catechistica* in your prayer. That is to say, that you take the biblical text of the next catechetical encounter and follow the following process:

a. Invoke the Holy Spirit to enlighten you and help you understand the Word.
b. Re-read the text several times slowly until it becomes clear and familiar to you. With a pencil, mark the words that are repeated, draw the character that stands out, try to discover the central message of the text. If you have any doubts, read the notes of the Bible, or look for a commentary. And if you still have doubts, write them down to consult with someone. But this first step consists in making the text clear, so that you can say what it is about, that you feel that you know it.
c. Then, begin to ask yourself what that message says to your own life; what the Lord wants to change in your own way of behaving, in your feelings, in your reactions, in your plans; what the Holy Spirit wants to polish and improve. If there is something that bothers you in that biblical text, do not fail to recognize it to ask yourself why and to talk about it with the Lord.

d. Ask the Lord for his grace to be able to respond to that Word, and imagine how you will be able to obey what the Lord asks of you.
e. Dedicate a few minutes to thanking the Lord, to adoring him, to contemplating him.
f. Then, think that that Word is also for others. So begin to remember your catechumens, and ask the Lord what he wants to say to them through that Word.

   Certainly, there will be some doctrinal content that you will have to explain to them, but you will always have to try to make that Word lead them to a personal encounter with the Lord, with his love, with his friendship. Try to discover what they will need to hear most when you explain that Word to them.
g. Pray to the Lord for them, so that they may receive the Word with an open heart.

THE SECRET IMPULSE OF THE SPIRIT

The catechist could simply seek immediate success, to feel important, skilled, or capable. But in that case, the fruits of his work will be superficial and fleeting. On the other hand, if he truly loves the catechumens and they are the important ones, then he will try to allow the Holy Spirit to act and let himself be carried away by the Spirit.

> Evangelization will never be possible without the action of the Holy Spirit....In fact, it is only after the coming of the Holy Spirit on the day of Pentecost that the apostles depart to all the ends of the earth in order to begin the great work of the Church's evangelization....
>
> It is He who explains to the faithful the deep meaning of the teaching of Jesus and of His mystery. It is the Holy Spirit who, today just as at the beginning of the Church, acts in every

> evangelizer who allows himself to be possessed and led by Him. The Holy Spirit places on his lips the words which he could not find by himself....
>
> Techniques of evangelization are good, but even the most advanced ones could not replace the gentle action of the Spirit. The most perfect preparation of the evangelizer has no effect without the Holy Spirit. Without the Holy Spirit the most convincing dialectic has no power over the heart of man. Without Him the most highly developed schemas resting on a sociological or psychological basis are quickly seen to be quite valueless...the Holy Spirit is the principal agent of evangelization: it is He who impels each individual to proclaim the Gospel, and it is He who in the depths of consciences causes the word of salvation to be accepted and understood. (EN 75)

It should not be forgotten that "supernatural" effectiveness or fruitfulness cannot be confused with the fame of the catechist, with the admiration he or she may arouse, or with the psychological effects or emotional reactions he or she may achieve.

The discreet action of the Spirit is rather characterized by the depth of its effects (generosity, self-giving, forgiveness, etc.) and by the stability of those effects in the lives of the catechumens, which last long beyond the presence of the catechist.

If he or she has a humble and firm trust in the action of the Spirit, the catechist can be more easily used by the

Spirit and experiences the fervor of sowing a seed that always acts by its own power:

> Let us therefore preserve our fervor of spirit. Let us preserve the delightful and comforting joy of evangelizing, even when it is in tears that we must sow. May it mean for us—as it did for John the Baptist, for Peter and Paul, for the other apostles and for a multitude of splendid evangelizers all through the Church's history—an interior enthusiasm that nobody and nothing can quench. May it be the great joy of our consecrated lives. (EN 80)

This attitude of trust in the Spirit is also an expression of love for people, because only the Spirit can work what the human heart needs:

> And may the world of our time, which is searching, sometimes with anguish, sometimes with hope, be enabled to receive the Good News not from evangelizers who are dejected, discouraged, impatient or anxious, but from ministers of the Gospel whose lives glow with fervor, who have first received the joy of Christ. (EN 80)

Sad and discouraged are the catechists who do not trust in the mysterious action of the Spirit. Impatient or anxious are those who trust too much in their own ability. They adore themselves, and that is why they need quick and visible successes.

When catechesis does not provide all the satisfactions that the person would like, when the fruits are smaller than expected, when the heart gets tired of fighting for the appearance and recognition of others, it is possible that new poisons will take over the catechist that destroy spiritual enthusiasm: skepticism, tiredness, discouragement.

It is when tiredness has turned into fatigue, into apathy, into meaninglessness, into sadness. When catechetical activity has already become like a job, as limited as possible, so as not to disturb a comfortable life. It is not the happy and serene tiredness of one who has given himself up for love in the catechetical encounter. The effort no longer makes sense. That means that the activity has lost its deepest motives, and then it is simply "endured." That activity is no longer spiritual. Catechesis has lost the "Spirit."

The catechist has tired himself out trying to prove that he is worth a lot, and he has not succeeded. So finally, he gives up and tells himself that it is no longer worth the effort, that everything is relative. In order to maintain himself in this state of apathy for which he has opted in the depths of his heart, he says to himself: "It all makes no difference." "My work does not bear fruit." "When catechesis ends, there is nothing left." "I do not have much to contribute." "Catechesis does not provide solutions to the problems of man today." "The world is going in other directions, and no matter how hard I try, I will not be able to row against the current." "What I can achieve is too small, at the cost of a very great effort."

This skepticism is a true suicide, it is a renunciation of fecundity, which at the same time is a renunciation of living. It is mutilating and atrophying the deepest core of the person more and more each day, which produces the most terrible spiritual death. There spirituality ends, no matter how much the person prays.

Therefore, it is good to remember some spiritual motivations that help us recover enthusiasm, fervor, drive, and confidence.

Let us remember (and contemplate in prayer) the example of the early Christian community, as it appears in the Acts and the Pauline letters. There we see Christians filled with the joy of the Spirit, with courage in proclamation, and capable of great active resistance. But all this sprang from the community encounter with the living, risen Lord. Faith allows us to believe God, who through that testimony tells us that it is possible to evangelize in that way. If in those difficult circumstances, in the midst of persecution, it was possible to proclaim love, courage, and joy, we can also live it today. But we must accept living it, we must dare to take that risk and that challenge that takes us out of our normality. It is good to reread some texts of the New Testament and meditate on them in prayer. It can be a great help against skepticism (Acts 4:13–31; 8:26–40; 2 Cor 5:13–15; Phil 4:1–8; 1 Thess 1:1–9).

If we become complex beings who believe that what the world offers has more power and beauty than the proposal of the gospel, let us ask ourselves: Does the world really offer anything better? Is politics really offering anything more to the world? Can individualistic consumerism create a better humanity? Can unlimited scientific and economic progress without moral limits ensure a future of justice, peace, and freedom?

It would be good to imagine what Saint Paul, Saint Augustine, Saint Francis of Assisi, or Mother Teresa of

Calcutta would tell us if we presented them with excuses to justify our discouragement, cowardice, and comforts.

Our discouragement is often cured when we see that there are still people today who let themselves be carried away by the Spirit, capable of giving their lives for a conviction, and above all that there are still catechist martyrs who give their lives for Jesus Christ and his gospel. If some can give themselves in such a way to a mission that involves giving their own blood, then comfort, mediocrity, and skeptical laziness have no more excuses. I, as a catechist, will have difficult moments, but I have not yet shed blood for Jesus Christ.

Faith is not only believing in God but also believing him, believing that it is true that he loves us, that he leads history, that he is capable of intervening, that he does not abandon us, that he brings good out of evil with his power and his infinite creativity. It is believing that he can always help us. It is believing in the presence of Jesus who marches victoriously in history with "those… called and chosen and faithful" (Rev 17:14), believing in the discreet but real action of the Spirit, believing in the intercession of the saints (Rev 6:9–10).

Hope is to have the certainty that we will always have at our disposal the help of God to move forward, to face everything and for everything to end well. Hope makes what we believe by faith become a certainty about our own lives and about this concrete history that we are living. The Lord who has already overcome the power of evil many times will continue to overcome (Rev 6:2). Because God does not dwell only in the small lights of the present, he also dwells in the future. That is why the future will not be without his glory and his saving presence.[4]

The Holy Spirit can act mysteriously in any circumstance, even in the midst of the apparent failures of catechesis. That is why Paul gloried in his weaknesses (2 Cor 12:10) where the power of grace was perfectly manifested (2 Cor 12:9).

Because "we have this treasure in clay jars, so that it may be made clear that this extraordinary power belongs to God and does not come from us" (2 Cor 4:7). This is what is called "a sense of mystery." It is knowing with certainty that whoever offers himself to God for love (Rom 12:1), and in that way surrenders himself to the mission that God entrusts to him, will surely be fruitful, will be a branch with abundant fruit (John 15:5), his life and his activity will not be sterile. No catechetical encounter will be useless.

Jesus said: "My Father is glorified by this, that you bear much fruit" (John 15:8). But these fruits are produced in a mysterious way, this fecundity is often invisible, unfathomable, cannot be counted. Therefore, the catechist can give himself intensely to the mission with the certainty that his effort will be fruitful, but without pretending to know how, where or when. That is "the secret of the Spirit."

None of our work done with love is lost, none of our sincere concern for others is lost, no act of love for God is lost, no generous fatigue is lost. All that goes on around the world as a force of life that bears fruit. Just as when we produce waves in the sea with the movement of our hands and that movement spreads throughout the ocean, in the same way no work done for love and with love will fail to change the universe. No catechetical encounter lived with love will be useless.

But it is important to learn to let yourself be loved even when you believe you have failed, to learn little by little to let yourself be in the tenderness of the Father's arms. We must learn to let ourselves be touched by grace, allowing God himself to console us, so that we do not renounce the ministry of pouring out consolation on others. The following text wonderfully expresses what we have just said:

> [God] consoles us in all our affliction, so that we may be able to console those who are in any affliction with the consolation with which we ourselves are consoled by God. For just as the sufferings of Christ are abundant for us, so also our consolation is abundant through Christ. If we are being afflicted, it is for your consolation and salvation; if we are being consoled, it is for your consolation, which you experience when you patiently endure the same sufferings that we are also suffering. Our hope for you is unshaken, for we know that as you share in our sufferings, so also you share in our consolation. (2 Cor 1:4–7)

All this is only possible by the grace of the Holy Spirit. Only the action of grace can heal our skepticism and our unhealthy discouragement, entering into the depths of our motivations and our energies. That is why it is necessary to invoke each day the action of the Holy Spirit to strengthen us internally, to give us once again the energy, the courage, the inexhaustible joy of evangelizing.

But moved by the Holy Spirit we must leave the comfortable shore and throw ourselves "into the deep" (Luke 5:1–11), overcoming our fears (Mark 4:35–41) with our eyes on Christ (Matt 14:22–33). It is worth the joy of telling others that "we have found the Messiah" (John 1:41).

When we let the Holy Spirit—who flows from the heart of the Risen One—impel us in this task, we will surely experience the wonders that he can do in hearts, and we will be amazed to see what his grace can accomplish. This is what Saint Paul experienced, who preached the gospel "not in word only but also in power and in the Holy Spirit and with full conviction" (1 Thess 1:5). Saint Peter also spoke of this precious gospel preached "by the Holy Spirit" (1 Pet 1:12). In this way the joy of the disciples of Emmaus is lived, who felt "their hearts burning" with Christ and therefore went out to communicate it to others: "the Lord has risen indeed" (Luke 24:34)!

The Holy Spirit can provoke here and there shoots of a new world. Even if they are cut off, those shoots will sprout again, because the resurrection of the Lord has already penetrated the hidden fabric of this history, because Jesus has not risen in vain. It is worth being a part of this dynamic of the Spirit with our catechetical mission.

Personal Journey

a. Enter into the presence of God, thank him and adore him for a moment.
b. Try to remember some moments when you have felt sad, discouraged, disillusioned, or lost the taste and joy of catechesis.
c. Ask yourself if any of that has remained in your heart. Write down everything you feel with total sincerity.

d. Begin to invoke the Holy Spirit insistently. Remember that he is a fire that purifies, that gives warmth, that illuminates, that burns away all that is bad. And ask him to destroy all the negative feelings that disturb you. Ask him to heal the bad memories, and to make a change inside you: that instead of discouragement he may put hope; that instead of sadness he may put joy; that instead of loneliness he may put friendship with Jesus; that instead of wounded pride he may put humility and simplicity.
e. Imagine how your next catechetical encounter would be if you had much more fervor, enthusiasm, joy, and confidence. And ask the Holy Spirit to do it.

THE PATIENCE OF LOVE

Spiritual growth is a process—generally slow—in which the grace of God works with the weak freedom of man, without violating it. The freedom of our catechumens is full of conditioning, obstacles, and wounds, which often diminish the responsibility for their actions.[5] The seeds of the Spirit also germinate in the midst of the weeds (cf. Matt 13:24–30) in a mysterious way that cannot always be rushed or measured by external criteria (cf. Mark 4:26–32). This conviction should be burned into the heart of the catechist, so that he can respect and patiently wait for the people's time.

In catechesis, the different virtues that allow us to adequately express love are put into play and prevent that love from weakening. One of those virtues is patience. Without patience there is no love, because "love is patient" (1 Cor 13:4).

When the catechist is unable to tolerate the defects of others, cannot bear that others modify his plans, or does not accept that they interrupt what he has projected and prepared, then he cares more about the task than the people. But since people do not allow themselves to be manipulated or absorbed, it is possible that soon certain activities will become a burden lived without joy. The lack of patience can thus cause a disorder in the catechetical activity, which ceases to be an expression and nourishment of spirituality and becomes only an external fulfillment that is tolerated with great difficulty.

If we have chosen to serve others, to help them carry the burdens of life, and to announce the gospel to them, we will need to be patient with them. We will have to tolerate their limits, accepting that they take away part of our time, that they contradict us, or that they do not listen to us. Because impatience not only ends up making us sick and destroying us inside; it also makes us enemies of those we should love.[6]

The lack of patience torments our soul with grudges and regrets, ruins our life, and sickens the heart of the catechist with feelings of sadness and discouragement. Others become detestable beings or, at best, tolerable.

The first thing that is required to be patient with someone is to give importance to that person, to value them deeply. If we feel like gods and believe that others are worthless, then we will be unable to tolerate their defects or mistakes, and nothing will prevent us from hurting them. Sometimes it happens that catechists, because they consider themselves more educated or more grown than others, tend to look at them as imperfect, ignorant, or "low-quality" beings. This certainly does not favor a sincere attitude of patience and understanding. The Word of God proposes the opposite:

> All of you must clothe yourselves with humility in your dealings with one another, for "God

> opposes the proud but gives grace to the humble." (1 Pet 5:5)

When the temptation arises to be intolerant or impatient with someone, the first thing to remember is that that person is a work of God, that God put all his love into creating them. That person does not exist by chance or by fate but because there is a love, the love of God, that has wanted to give them existence and sustains their being at every moment. That person exists because God, from all eternity, thought of giving them life. Their life has meaning because it is part of God's plan. So, they have a place in the universe, even though I may not be able to discover it. They have the right to be here, just like me.

But there is something deeper: God, in giving life to that person, created them in his image. This means that they have an immense dignity, because God is reflected in their being, even though I may not be able to recognize it. On the other hand, God lives in that person, dwells in their interior. If it were not for that permanent presence of God, that person would not exist.

Thus, recognizing the greatness of that human being, it is more possible that we can be patient with their weaknesses and defects. True patience is a deep spiritual attitude.

We can also be more patient with someone if we try to recognize and appreciate the good things that that person has. No person is pure darkness, no one is only defects and nothing more than defects. God does not do horrible or useless things. If we think that it is really God who created that person, then we cannot think that they do not have something valuable. We may not have discovered it. Sometimes it is envy that prevents us from recognizing the good things in some people. But the Holy Spirit sows in all human beings some charisms: in some it will be sympathy, or a beautiful smile; in others it will be the ability to sing well, or some other ability. The Spirit also sows good habits: a person can be aggressive but very responsible, or they can be a thief but very compassionate with their family. The defects that someone has do not mean that everything else that is in that person is false. It is important to try to look carefully to discover those good things that allow us to improve the image we have of that person. If we don't succeed, we can ask their mother or their friends. But we can also ask the Holy Spirit to enlighten us to see how it is working in that person, in the midst of the defects that bother us. In this way, we can recognize that that person is not pure darkness. They are a mixture of light and darkness, of bad things and good things.

If we look at ourselves, we can discover that we are also a mixture. We are not pure light, pure goodness, pure generosity, pure selflessness. But neither are we pure evil and selfishness. Knowing this allows us to not hate ourselves, and then we do not need to reject others.[7]

A practice that can be very useful is imagining what the bothersome person will be like when they are in heaven. There they will no longer have defects or blemishes, or bad attitudes. There they will be freed and healed from all that. In heaven that person will be perfectly restored by God and will shine with all the beauty that God wanted to give them, full of love and kindness.

Thus, transformed by God, we are both called to live together eternally in heaven. We will not cease to be ourselves, but we will shine free from all imperfection and from everything unpleasant.

Another spiritual resource for having more patience is to stop and contemplate the patience of God:

> The Lord is not slow about his promise, as some think of slowness, but is patient with you, not wanting any to perish....Regard the patience of our Lord as salvation. (2 Pet 3:9, 15)

God respects the freedom and times of each person, to the point of tolerating being offended in many ways, patiently allowing himself to be ignored and despised. Within this sinful humanity, it is very important that I also recognize the patience that God has had with me in many moments of my existence, when I made my plans and projects outside of his plan for my life, without consulting him. Or when I resisted his love and the joy that he wanted to give me; the times that I closed myself off in my grudges, selfishness, and sadness. However, God always had patience with me, he waited for me with tenderness and offered me his friendship freely. Therefore, he expects me to act with others in the same way. But this is not about mortifying oneself with guilt, because this can translate into intolerance with others to compensate for one's own feelings of inferiority. It is about the authentic tenderness of one who feels that he has been lovingly understood and waited for. Then he can be compassionate with others. If we value the patient and loving waiting of God with us, we can avoid being anxious about the slowness of the changes in others. Because changes in behavior depend on deep inner transformations, and sometimes take many years (and if we talk about cultures, we have to think in decades and centuries). Normally visible changes take place slowly, with small steps. Impatient evangelizers cannot bear this and then live disgusted with others. In addition, there are people who begin to change only when they feel accepted as they are, with all their virtues and defects; when they know that someone loves them and waits with affection, without anxiety. But when they feel that someone wants to dominate them or impose an immediate change on them, they resist inside and decide to remain as they are.

Sometimes we think that the model of God is too perfect for us to imitate. We forget that the Son of God has become man like us, and truly shared in our whole existence. He was a healthy, free human being. He could react with firmness, as when he confronted the religious people of his time, who hurt the weak and controlled the lives of others (Matt 23:23; Luke 11:46). But he was extremely patient with sinners, the imperfect, the unfaithful. He was also patient while he was being insulted and crucified (Luke 23:33–34). That is why he could say: "[L]earn from me; for I am gentle and humble in heart, and you will find rest for your souls" (Matt 11:29). Because the impatient have no rest, they find no calm. They are always disturbed by the mistakes and defects of others and therefore cannot have a serene heart. On the other hand, those who learn to look with tenderness on the imperfections of others find inner serenity and stop being so disturbed when others make mistakes. Jesus said: "Blessed are the meek" (Matt 5:5). It is good to contemplate Jesus's patience, to imagine his serene heart when people invaded him and changed his plans (Mark 6:31–34; Matt 14:13–14). We can also notice his compassionate gaze on the miseries and mistrusts of his disciples (Mt 14:30–31; 20:20–23), his love so human and divine.

We can ask the Holy Spirit to work its grace within us, so that we can be more like Jesus in his way of acting and have some of his patience and compassion.

The model of Jesus becomes more luminous in his passion:

> Christ also suffered for you, leaving you an example, so that you should follow in his steps....When he was abused, he did not return abuse; when he suffered, he did not threaten. (1 Pet 2:21, 23)

In the passion of Christ, we can see that the person we dislike has a great value. To discover how much he or she is worth in the eyes of God, it is convenient to remember what the Father God gave for that person: the precious blood of his own Son. That is why the Bible says: "You were bought with a price" (1 Cor 7:23). He "obtained with the blood of his own Son" (Acts 20:28). Therefore, we can recognize that that person is worth so much, that the price paid for him or her is the life of Jesus offered on the cross.

Therefore, when I look at that face that bothers me, I can imagine Jesus suffering in that human being. Instead of being attentive to what I dislike, I can contemplate in that person the face of Jesus crowned with thorns. Thus I will also be able to endure some injustice without feeding grudges.

Let us also remember that when one believes in God and loves him, one is also called to offer him something.

Sometimes we can offer to God things that we ourselves choose: a fast, alms, or any other sacrifice. But in reality what pleases God most is that we offer those things that are part of everyday life. For example: the attitudes of others that sometimes take away our patience, everything that bothers us about others, be it big or small. God does not leave a sincere and generous offering unrewarded. He is not interested in offerings made from the mouth out, but in his infinite love he values the offerings of our heart, those that spring from a true decision. As when we accept having to put up with someone who has a character we don't like, or who talks in an irritating way, or who thinks in a different way.

But a catechist, if he or she is truly in love with his or her mission, is capable of offering those annoyances for the very people to whom he or she has been sent, so that they may attain the fullness and happiness that God wants for them.

We know that there is no true patience if the heart is full of resentment. But to overcome resentment, we must try to find some excuse for that person, something that will help us to understand and forgive him or her for that way of acting, so that we do not feel attacked when he or she says or does something unpleasant. That is how Jesus reacted when he was crucified: "Father, forgive them; for they do not know what they are doing" (Luke 23:34). It is healthy to think that perhaps that person reacts that way because of some deep sufferings that he or she keeps in his or her heart, because of some memories that torture him or her, because of a feeling of inferiority that poisons him or her, because he or she has been hurt a lot in the past, or because life denied him or her what he or she wanted most. By looking for those excuses, it is possible to learn to look with tenderness and compassion at his or her defects and bad attitudes.

Sometimes what makes us impatient with others is anxiety, that "nervousness" that is a kind of permanent inner hurry. The anxious person may appear serene on the outside, but on the inside they are accelerated. They feel an imperious need to achieve everything immediately. They want to finish everything he or she has to do quickly, without leaving anything pending; They need to anticipate everything. So, their mind always goes further ahead than his or their body. When they are doing something, they are thinking about what they will have to do next. They do not focus on anything in depth, they are not with their whole being in any task or in any thing. They do not dedicate all their attention to the people they deal with. They listen to them thinking about what they will have to answer or what they will have to do next. In this way, they deprive themselves of authentic relationships, and others become a simple means to carry out their projects.

It is better to give ourselves fully to each thing we have to do, thinking only about that and leaving the future or tomorrow in the hands of the Lord. It is better that God be the king and the Lord of our task, that he guide our activity, and everything will end well, although many things will surprise us and catch us unprepared.

It is true that God's plans can take us on other paths that we would not have dreamed of, but it will always be for our good. Therefore, it is better to be able to stop with all our being in the catechetical activity, discovering its value:

> I saw that there is nothing better than that all should enjoy their work, for that is their lot. (Eccl 3:22)

Especially in the things we do for God, we have to let go of the fruits. When the results come, it is good to stop and enjoy them, with a heart grateful to God, who has made us fruitful. But when the fruits do not come, it is better to be patient remembering that God will gather the fruits at his time, in his time, and for his glory. Jesus already said that when we finish a task we have to say, "We are worthless slaves; we have done only what we ought to have done!" (Luke 17:10). But the person who has been dominated by anxiety lives pending the fruit of his or her work, and when he or she achieves it, he or she does not enjoy it for long, because he or she soon needs to obtain something more, something new. Vanity leads us to be anxious while awaiting the fruits, but love leads us to surrender ourselves to work with all our soul to fulfill a mission, detached from our personal glory and leaving the results in the hands of God. Because "unless the Lord builds the house, those who build it labor in vain" (Ps 127:1).

Finally, let us also contemplate Mary. After having searched for Jesus for two days everywhere, she finally found him in the temple and told him of the anguish she had gone through. But Jesus answered her that she should be about her Father's business (Luke 2:41–49). She did not understand what that meant concretely (Luke 2:50), but she accepted with patience that divine mystery that surpassed her, those plans of God that she could not yet encompass. Therefore, despite not being able to control the situation with her mind, she "treasured all these things in her heart" (Luke 2:51). Patience, someday the light would bring understanding. Also in the catechetical task many things escape our control, our planning, and our structures, but many times we have to surrender ourselves with the patience of love to the mysterious projects of God, which are not always our own.

Personal Journey

a. Enter the presence of Jesus and thank him for the patience he has had with you throughout your life, because many times he has understood you and has waited for you.

b. Contemplate the patience of Jesus on the cross and thank him from the heart. Perhaps you can kiss a crucifix and express in that kiss all your love and gratitude.

c. Remember the moments when you have lost your patience, even if it is only internally, with one of your catechumens. But don't blame yourself or them. Just contemplate the scenes.

d. Ask Jesus to take you with his love, with his tenderness, with his compassion, with his gaze. Try to find some explanation for the behavior or way of being of that person. Try to look at them as Jesus would look at them, imagine yourself reacting as Jesus would react.

e. Stop to ask the Lord for the grace to react like that in the future, trying to overcome evil with good.

f. Surrender the control of your task to the Holy Spirit. Try to make a deep renunciation saying something like: "Lord, I no longer want to have everything under my control. I give you the fruits of my work. I want to work only for love, knowing that the fruits will come in their time, even if I do not see them. Heal my impatience, beloved Lord."

TENDERNESS THAT ADAPTS

When the document *Redemptoris missio* refers to the "spirit" of evangelizing action, it places a strong emphasis on love, so that in everything we do or decide we adapt to what is convenient for others:

> Love, which has been and remains the driving force of mission, and is also "the sole criterion for judging what is to be done or not done, changed or not changed. It is the principle which must direct every action, and end to which that action must be directed. When we act with a view to charity, or are inspired by charity, nothing is unseemly and everything is good." (RMi 60)

Therefore, catechesis should always be an expression of close fraternal love, avoiding everything that could hurt, offend, or humiliate others. Catechists should also avoid speaking to others as those who live far from their difficulties and anxieties. The framework of a loving catechesis will always be made up of "concern, tenderness, compassion, openness, availability, and interest in people's problems." Because the catechist must first of all announce to others "that they are loved by God and are capable of loving" (RMi 89).

God, who speaks to the catechist in his Word, also speaks to them through reality. Attentive to what happens to others, they will be able to discover what they must announce in a given context and in a given way. In that context it is God himself who has something to say to his people. The question is: What does God want to say to these people, with this Word, in this concrete circumstance?

> In fact there are innumerable events in life and human situations which offer the opportunity for a discreet but incisive statement of what the Lord has to say in this or that particular circumstance. It suffices to have true spiritual sensitivity for reading God's message in events. (EN 43)

Let us note that this pedagogical attitude is called "*spiritual* sensitivity."

The circumstances—the things that the catechumens are living—"present a certain challenge to our capacity for discovery and adaptation" (EN 40). What we are saying is what Bl. Enrique Angelelli called "putting an ear to the people." The catechist has received the Word and has allowed it to touch their life, but they receive it to communicate it to a human group in a given circumstance.

Here the fraternal attitudes of spirituality come into play, which awaken our sensitivity to recognize what others need to hear, to discover the human situations where that Word can be poured out as light and as an answer: the concerns, anxieties, desires, and questions of the catechumens.

Both recent events and basic human experiences (disappointments, fear of loneliness, insecurity about the future, emotional dissatisfaction, concern for a loved one, etc.) can be taken into account, which in some way affect all people. In other words, the things that the catechumens have lived or are living.

Thus, by trying to "diligently seek signs of God's will and impulses of his grace in the various events of life" (PO 18), one comes to discover "what the Lord has to say in this or that particular circumstance" (EN 43).

It is about contemplating the lives of others with the eyes of God to seek the basic motivation that helps to awaken interest in the Word that is proclaimed, so that preaching does not answer questions that no one asks.

But this attitude of adaptation to others also implies two permanent concerns in the catechist:

> Respect for the religious and spiritual situation of those being evangelized. Respect for their tempo and pace; no one has the right to force them excessively. Respect for their conscience and convictions, which are not to be treated in a harsh manner. Another sign of this love is concern not to wound the other person, especially if he or she is weak in faith [Rom 14:15], with statements that may be clear for those who are already initiated but which for

> the faithful can be a source of bewilderment and scandal, like a wound in the soul. (EN 79)

This attitude allows us to love and value the way of life and belief of the catechumens and their families. Therefore, the presentation of the evangelical message will not be an imposition but a response to the concerns present in them. Also in the small world of their catechumens, the catechist will try to carry out a process of "inculturation"[8] as has been indicated precisely in *Catechesi tradendae*: "Inculturation" takes place when the gospel penetrates a place in such a way that it moves the culture of that place to produce "original expressions" of Christian life (CT 53a). This is realized when catechesis in a place manages to make "from its depths" (GS 58d) new Christian cultural expressions, when the spirituality of the gospel becomes "passion" in a group of people, when it spontaneously awakens a favorable sensitivity.[9] The spirituality of the catechist includes that zeal to incarnate the gospel in the sensitivity of their catechumens, as they are, as they feel, as they live.[10]

When Saint Bonaventure spoke of those things that can help a sinner return to the path of God, he mentioned a "piety inserted in the entrails from childhood" (II Sent 28, 2, 1). When maternal education, catechesis, and popular culture have succeeded in producing a deep religious sentiment, this intimate piety becomes a permanent attraction that, in the sinful person, can be used by the Spirit to seduce the heart and initiate the return to friendship with God. In this sense, it is important to emphasize the importance of Christian signs that impregnate the culture of the poor, producing a spontaneous transmission of faith and Christian life. The catechist should nurture a sensitivity to recognize the signs that can help the catechumens to express and sustain their faith.

In my case, for example, I can mention something that God has frequently used to reach my life with his grace, showing me his glory and inviting me to a personal encounter. It is an image of the Sacred Heart in the church of my town, where, since my childhood, I frequently experienced the call to intimacy with God. This happened thanks to a catechist who invited me to look at that image in the eyes, without fear, recognizing the love of Jesus for me. Even today, even in moments of great aridity, when I pass by the church of my town and stop for a moment in front of that image, the desire to love God more, the gratitude for the friendship he offers me, and hope, among other things, are awakened in me.

In the life of each one of us are these "personal sacramentals": things, places, songs, images that God often uses in a particular way so that we may recover the meaning of our life, the desire to give ourselves, the joy of his friendship. It is good, then, to remember that God has put wonderful signs on our personal path. Returning to those places, listening to that song again, meeting again with that sign that God uses can sometimes be—especially in difficult moments—the best resources to prevent a spiritual void from occurring in our life, to keep the flame of love burning.

The monk Anselm Grün has developed the value of personal "rituals," presenting the appearance of these rituals, which each one creates, as a necessary sacramental expression that reflects the authenticity of love for God and helps to recover the deep and joyful meaning of everyday activity:

> I have an allergic reaction when someone dreams of loving God very much, but in his concrete life nothing of that love for God is visible....If our relationship with Jesus Christ is authentic, it is seen in the way we organize our day, and for this the first hours of the morning are decisive. Morning rituals decide...whether we are motivated by the deadlines set for our tasks or whether we put everything we do under the blessing of God....A morning ritual that motivates for today awakens the energies that are enclosed in each one of us.[11]

When the catechist is able to recognize and create in their life those signs that help to sustain their own friendship with God, they will also be able to help the catechumens be enriched with some very personal signs that will accompany and help them throughout their lives. Even if they stop going to Mass for a while, they will leave catechesis loaded with signs that will help them to find God and return to him.

This process is slow, and it means not clinging so much to the plans, structures and multitude of contents that one sometimes insists on transmitting. Spiritual tenderness leads the catechist to renounce many times things they would like to say or teach, in order to adapt to the rhythm of the catechumens, to take advantage of something they have said, to stop before a gesture of theirs that can serve as a starting point. Spiritual tenderness makes us adaptable to the unpredictable and extremely respectful, in order to let Christian gestures emerge from the depths of the lives of the catechumens (from their mentality, their emotions, their way of expressing themselves), in order to help them find their own way of being Christians.

This supposes a very deeply rooted spiritual attitude, which allows one to react in time when new shoots of imposition or domination appear in the heart of the catechist. All this is part of adaptation to others and the delicacy of love.

Personal Journey

When we spoke of prayer with the Word, we saw that the catechist also asks himself or herself in prayer what the Lord wants to say to their catechumens with that Word. Now let us try to deepen this search by praying for a moment with their lives, trying to discover what they most need to hear.

a. Reading the biblical text in the presence of the Lord, try to contemplate your catechumens with love, remembering things they have told you about themselves, or gestures they have made, or attitudes and behaviors that help you discover what is happening to them, what worries them, what concerns them.
b. Then, try to discover what the biblical text you are meditating on can say to those concrete lives; ask yourself where that Word wants to be deposited in order to be a true light in their lives.
c. Take a moment to intercede for them, so that they may recognize what that Word wants to say to their concrete lives, so that

they may accept it and allow themselves to be transformed, consoled, and encouraged.

d. Try to remember some situations in which, perhaps without realizing it, you have wanted to impose on them some of your own ideas, tastes, and ways of thinking, without realizing that the Lord wanted to tell them something else, that they needed to hear something else, or that they needed to hear it in a different way. And ask the Lord for the grace to have a great sensitivity to adapt to them, to their way of expressing themselves, of feeling, of praying.

e. Invent in prayer some signs that will help you remember the Lord's love throughout each day, so that you can recognize the Lord more and make him present in your daily life.

f. Finally, try to imagine what signs could be transmitted to your catechumens by adapting to their sensitivity. Thus, when the catechetical encounter arrives, you will be able to help them find their own way of expressing their friendship with Jesus or the message that the Word has communicated to them.

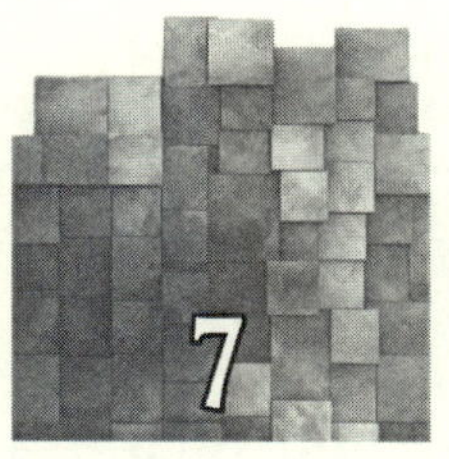

ALONE BEFORE THE POOR

To be spiritual and contemplative is also to learn to stop before others, loving them, perceiving their immense and sacred value. To contemplate is to be able to recognize, with deep attention, the immense dignity of every human being. It is to appreciate with sincere interest and affection the sparks of God that exist in each person.

But if we only exercise ourselves to stop before what is harmonious and beautiful according to the schemes of consumer society, we will only be able to stop before a beautiful, proportionate, clean, and healthy body. We will become selective beings, we will pretend to choose who to love, and then we will become more and more selfish, blind, and dissatisfied. Thus we will be absolutely incapable of stopping before the poor and sharing our life and our heart with them.

The wisdom of the Bible teaches us that in this way we will deprive ourselves of the deepest happiness, we will remain on the surface. We will feel mystical because we can stop before nature or before relaxing music, but in reality our interior will remain far from external reality, incapable of stopping before the true world. This unhealthy deception is revealed if we read some biblical advice:

> When you give a luncheon or a dinner, do not invite your friends or your brothers and sisters or your relatives or rich neighbors, in case they may invite you in return, and you would be repaid. But when you give a banquet, invite the poor, the crippled, the lame, and the blind. And you will be blessed because they cannot repay you, for you will be repaid at the resurrection of the righteous. (Luke 14:12–14)

"And you will be happy!" says Jesus. What mysterious secret of happiness is there here? What discreet and delicate light does the Lord want us to discover from this advice?

In another biblical text, it is told that Jesus knelt to wash the feet of his disciples. After doing so, he asked them to learn to wash one another's feet, and concluded by saying: "If you know these things, you are blessed if you do them" (John 13:17). Again Jesus offers a strange secret of happiness: "You are blessed if you do them."

Already in the Old Testament this mysterious promise was found. The prophet Isaiah invited us to share bread with the hungry, to welcome the poor into our own home, and to cover the naked, and then he spoke of the consequences of all this: "Then your light shall break forth like the dawn, and your healing shall spring up quickly" (Isa 58:8).

In what self-help manual do these curious secrets of health and happiness appear?

In reality, these biblical texts help us to unmask the false techniques of happiness that do not reach to truly satisfy the problems of the heart. The intimacy of the human being only matures in generous love and is not happy until it learns to love seriously.

The people who have chosen to "live with" the poor and disabled, who not only give them some material help but also share their lives with them, teach us this art of stopping before them to reach the deepest joy.

I would like to mention the testimony of Jean Vanier as an example. Vanier emphasizes how in this competitive world, "to be a friend is to make oneself vulnerable, to drop the masks and barriers in order to welcome the other as he is, with his beauty, his gifts, his limits and his sufferings." There, in the loving encounter, especially when the other is suffering or disabled, it is not about "ascending in rank, becoming more and more efficient and seeking recognition, but about descending, about wasting my time."[12]

But it is interesting to hear Vanier's testimony when he explains how that unique happiness that the Bible promises to those who are able to stop with love before the poor and suffering began to be born in him:

> I felt new currents of tenderness arise in me when, by touching the fragility and suffering of people with disabilities, I received their trust. I loved them and I felt happy with them. They awakened a part of my being that, until then, was underdeveloped, atrophied. They

> opened the door to another world for me, not the world of strength and success, power and efficiency, but the world of the heart, vulnerability and communion. And this was new for me. They led me on a path of healing and inner unity.[13]

Let us also read some more palpable examples of this type of superior joy, of this way of "stopping" before a poor or disabled person that provokes a happy liberation:

> Sometimes Loïc sits on my knees. Small, poor, unable to speak despite his forty years, he is there, silent. He looks at me and I look at him. We are in communion with each other....With people with mental disabilities like Loïc, we live these moments of contemplation, full of silence and peace. He looks at me and I look at him. Moments of healing that unify body and spirit. By identifying with the poor, Jesus reminds us that he identifies with the little child in each of us. The important thing is to be trusting, open, and amazed like a child. Each person is sacred, whatever their disability, their fragility, their culture.[14]

However, it is not an idyll, because the relationship with those who suffer is not always a serene contemplation shared. Sometimes one must learn to recognize one's own reactions and weaknesses in order to avoid withdrawing again into the inner world, because "this withdrawal into oneself leads to an asphyxiation of the heart."[15]

But the simple fact of turning universal love into a true ideal, into an inner passion, already frees us from a false contemplation, or from an apparent peace, because our most intimate fibers are made for universal love, to feel that "every human being is my brother," to stop before others.

Every "spiritual" person is capable of "lowering himself" like Jesus to stop before the other, who is worthy of his love, to recognize the good in him, to listen to him, to ask him for an opinion, and to help him without feeling superior. It is not for nothing that Saint Paul made this exhortation: "in humility regard others as better than yourselves" (Phil 2:1–4). And Jesus warned us that "all who exalt themselves will be humbled" (Luke 14:11).

Catechesis is also made up of some profound moments "alone" with one of the catechumens, especially with those who have difficulties, with those who are most in need of love, with the most complicated, with the most suffering, with the most limited. These moments alone should become moments of deep loving contemplation, where the other is sacred, is contemplated as an image of God, as a beloved son of the Father, as called to the happiness of heaven, as immensely valuable, contemplated with the love with which Jesus looks at him.

It is worth remembering some moments. For example, when Jesus met the deaf-mute, "He took him aside in private, away from the crowd, and put his fingers into his ears, and he spat and touched his tongue" (Mark 7:33). Or when Jesus was face-to-face with the blind man and asked him: "What do you want me to do for you?" (Mark 10:51). Perhaps the most intense and beautiful spiritual moments of a catechist occur when he manages to be face-to-face with the naked reality of a catechumen, trying to interpret what he needs most so that he can find it in Jesus, his savior.

Personal Journey

a. When the next catechetical meeting is over, ask one of your catechumens to stay for a moment. But let it be the one you think is least gifted, least beautiful, least interesting. The one you think is the "poorest" of them all.
b. Try to have a moment of contemplative dialogue with that person, recognizing Jesus in him, discovering Christ crucified suffering within him and loving.
c. Take an interest in his things, try to help him express what interests him, what he likes, what is happening to him.
d. Try to make your gaze more and more like that of Jesus, giving great importance to everything he tells you, looking at his face with attention and paying all your interest to his person, as if you two were the only ones who exist in the universe.
e. Afterward, stay alone with the Lord for a moment, remembering this catechumen and speaking to Jesus about him, thanking him and asking him for the needs you have discovered. But above all, remembering his face and recognizing in him the image of God, his immense nobility as a beloved son of the Father.

THE SUMMIT AND THE SOURCE

If the Eucharist is the summit and source of the life of the Church, it is also the summit and source of catechetical activity. The catechist brings the work done to the Eucharist and offers it to God. At the same time, he seeks to heal what has not been well lived in the catechesis and seeks the nourishment to give himself more in his task.

When the catechist goes to Mass and approaches to receive Communion, he does not merely live an encounter with Christ individually, but he is burdened by the presence of his catechumens in his heart.

Jesus in the Eucharist teaches us what it means to love, to what extent we have to become one with others:

> To become one in everything that others desire, even in the smallest and most insignificant things, in which one perhaps does not even pay attention, but which are important for others. Jesus exemplified this way of acting precisely by instituting the Eucharist.... To

> become one to the point of letting oneself be eaten! That is love.
>
> To become one in such a way that others feel nourished by our love, comforted, relieved, understood.[16]

Therefore, the catechist seeks in the Eucharist the strength that will allow him to give himself unreservedly to his mission, turning his life into food for others.

When he adores Jesus in the Eucharist, the catechist leaves his catechumens in the hands of the Lord. At the same time that he directs intense acts of love to Jesus, he cannot avoid incorporating his catechumens into that encounter. The attitude of surrendering them to the Lord, of asking for their needs, of offering his communion for them, of surrendering himself as an instrument so that that life of grace may reach them, spontaneously springs up in him.

In his adoration, he discovers that Jesus is the true Lord, the only one who deserves to be adored. That means that when he stops to adore him, he is contemplating someone who loves him, he is standing before the burning furnace overflowing with infinite love. Thus he discovers that the important thing is that the catechumens do not fall in love with his person but with Jesus; what matters is that they learn to adore him.

In adoration, he rediscovers that he is standing before the only Lord, who is the center of the universe, the center of his life, and the only center of his catechetical mission. We need to let ourselves be illuminated by his presence so that our mission and our whole life may be transfigured, until everything has a luminous meaning.

Because in the Eucharist our human heart finds the answers it needs in any circumstance:

> The eucharistic bread is the strength of the weak, the support of the sick, the balm that heals wounds, the help for those who leave this world. It is the vigor of the faithful who work in environments and circumstances in which their presence is the only possibility of proclaiming the Gospel.[17]

Saint Thomas Aquinas already taught that the Eucharist is a remedy for fragility; it gives vigor and vitality (ST III 65). It is not enough for him to sustain us, but it makes us grow and renews us (ST III 79). It is food not to help us survive but to "live" with enthusiasm, with intensity, with strength, with a healthy and happy impulse. Because it already begins to introduce us into the fullness of heaven as a "luminous star" and "makes fountains of energy spring up in the depths of the soul."[18]

He, from the Eucharist, attracts us and invites us to something more, he invites us to enter, to burn ourselves sweetly in his fire that gives life. Therefore, the adoration of Jesus in the Eucharist cannot be an end in itself. If that adoration is authentic, it must lead us to the irresistible desire for communion, it must lead us to the longing for fusion, to the search for the full union that can only take place in communion, to associate ourselves with Christ with all that we are and pass with him from death to life.

It is not enough to adore him in the tabernacle and experience his spiritual presence in our hearts, because it is not enough for him to transmit a spiritual force from there. He is food that waits to be eaten:

> In the Eucharist Jesus gives everything....God desires to be completely united to us so that all his being and ours can be fused in an eternal love. The whole long history of the relationship of God with human beings is a story of communion that is becoming ever deeper. It is not simply a story of unions, separations and reunions, but a story in which God seeks ever new ways of uniting in intimate communion with those who have been created in his image and likeness.[19]

He does not need to be present in the Eucharist. If he is there, it is to be food for the human heart, because he desires to be eaten and to be present in our lives, where he can love and be loved.

From this experience, the catechist will try to guide his catechumens toward the full encounter with Jesus in the Eucharist. He knows that something will always be missing as long as they sincerely and spontaneously desire the encounter with Jesus in communion.

In the celebration of the Eucharist, the whole mystery of the Passover of Jesus Christ is made present. In each Mass, the mystery of the cross is truly made present. Not because Christ dies again, since that perfect sacrifice of love is not repeated, but because that unique sacrifice of Christ is made present, it is actualized in a mysterious way. In fact, the risen Christ retains the marks of his nails, the signs of his surrender to the end (John 20:27; Rev 1:7; 5:6–9).

Moreover, Saint Paul presents the Christian experience as a participation in the passion of Christ: "I have been crucified with Christ...who loved me and gave himself for me" (Gal 2:19–20; 6:14–17; Col 1:24). In the Eucharist, "you proclaim the Lord's death until he comes" (1 Cor 11:26).

Our catechetical task is also, inevitably, a succession of deaths (renunciations, endings, surrenders, losses, stages that culminate). But the Eucharist allows us to associate ourselves in a very special way with the mystery of Christ who was given up, limited, made a sacrifice and an offering of love on the cross. And so, by uniting our wounds with his, we can give a mystical and ardent meaning to our own deaths, so that from those very deaths new life can spring forth.

That is why, in the Eucharist, the catechist can present all his or her weariness, worries, failures, humiliations, efforts, and pain. And all those crosses, united to the Passion of the Lord, become fruitful; they become a blessing for his or her catechumens.

But the Eucharist is not only a participation in the death of the Lord, since "if Christ has not been raised, your faith is futile, and you are still in your sins" (1 Cor 15:17). The wine, as in any banquet, also symbolizes the joy, the feast, and the vital fullness of the Risen Lord who communicates his happy life to us. And this is even more accentuated in the Sunday celebration, on the day when Christ conquered death and shares the joy of his triumph with his beloved Church. That is why the catechist also brings the joys of his or her task to the Mass and celebrates them. And he or she also brings the joys and the growth of his or her catechumens to celebrate them in the Eucharist.

Let us think that the Risen Christ is always present in the Church, but we have not yet fully reached in our lives that mystery of his new life, we have not completely passed from death to life. The Eucharist is "for us." In such a way that when we participate in the Eucharist, what happens to us is that we pass a little more, with Christ, from death to life. In that unique and supreme presence of the mystery of Easter, the life of grace that fills the overflowing heart of the Risen One is poured out on us. Thus we can attain something more of the divine life that reigns in the Risen One and abandon a little more the death that still dominates us. In this way, we become more and more instruments of life for the catechumens.

When the priest raises the host as an offering, he also raises with it the love, hopes, weariness, dreams and joys, the life of the people. There is also all the life that is growing in catechesis: the formation, the efforts to better prepare catechesis, the catechetical encounters, the entire life of the catechumens. And in the consecration, that life with all its richness is filled with the presence of Christ who illuminates it and makes it fruitful. In this way, by welcoming the presence of Christ and raising ourselves with him as instruments of love, each one of us becomes a channel of the eucharistic power so that the gospel and the life of grace may be poured out on catechesis with power and joy.

Personal Journey

I propose that you prepare yourself to live the next Mass well as a catechist. You could do it in the following way:

a. Go to the church a little before the Mass to adore Jesus and place him at the center of your own life.
b. In that moment alone with Jesus, tell him about the difficulties, the disappointments, the weariness of the catechetical task, and ask him to heal all that, to console, to liberate. And in this prayer, unite yourself to Jesus who gives himself up on the cross. Then, ask him to guide the Mass that is going to be celebrated so that it can be a true source of living water that will resurrect you with him, that will restore everything that has been damaged and fertilize your mission.
c. Then thank Jesus for all the good things you have experienced in catechesis. Remember that the Mass is also like the top of a mountain, where one arrives after a hard climb. So, offer Jesus all the efforts, all the attempts you have made to be a good catechist, every small act of love, and give it to Jesus as a gift of friendship.
d. Remember your catechumens one by one, and give them to Jesus in the tabernacle.
e. Then, in the celebration of the Mass, each moment will be lived with the heart of a catechist. In the penitential act you will ask for forgiveness for your lack of patience, for your negligence in preparing for the meetings, for your lack of joy in the mission, among other things. In the offerings you will give Jesus your catechumens, along with the

bread and wine. In the communion you will ask Jesus to bless your task with his grace and to nourish your enthusiasm, and so forth. Thus you will not cease to be a catechist in the celebration of the Mass. You will live the Mass with spiritual depth, and you will live it as a catechist.

IN LOVING COMMUNION

In his letter *Novo millennio ineunte*, Saint John Paul II particularly asked that Christians be educated in a "spirituality of communion":

> Before making practical plans, we need *to promote a spirituality of communion*, making it the guiding principle of education wherever individuals and Christians are formed. (NMI 43)

Therefore, this fraternal spirituality should occupy an important space in all catechesis. But that implies that catechists live this spirituality of communion among themselves. Today it is indispensable to always form a true educational community that is imbued with community spirit and that is open to a wider ecclesial community.

The pope does not limit himself to recalling the commandment of love, or to exhorting us to live it in our daily lives. He asks rather that the whole organization and planning of the Church's activity be effectively marked by this fraternal love:

> If we have truly contemplated the face of Christ, dear Brothers and Sisters, our pastoral planning will necessarily be inspired by the "new commandment" which he gave us: "Love one another, as I have loved you" (Jn 13:34). (NMI 42)

This implies revising our conception of the Church and imagining it as a welcoming home where everyone can live as brothers and sisters and constantly learn to be better brothers and sisters: "To make the Church *the home and the school of communion*: that is the great challenge facing us in the millennium which is now beginning" (NMI 43). All catechesis should be at the service of this objective.

But in explaining what this fraternity consists of, the pope avoids understanding it in an overly external way, only seeing it as unity in the confession of the same faith, or as an integration into certain structures, or as an agreement to develop joint activities with greater efficiency. Nor does he fall into the opposite extreme of exalting the intimate relationship with God. Here the pope refers to something intermediate, which is called "spirituality of communion," giving primacy to a series of evangelical attitudes toward the neighbor. To avoid reducing this spirituality to an emotional or purely subjective experience, he also stops to describe some concrete attitudes of this spirituality of communion:

> A spirituality of communion indicates above all the heart's contemplation of the mystery of the Trinity dwelling in us, and whose light we must also be able to see shining on the face of the brothers and sisters around us. A spirituality of communion also means an ability to think of our brothers and sisters in faith within the profound unity of the Mystical Body, and therefore as "those who are a part of me." This makes us able to share their joys and sufferings, to sense their desires and attend to their needs, to offer them deep and genuine friendship. A spirituality of communion implies also the ability to see what is positive in others, to welcome it and prize it as a gift from God: not only as a gift for the brother or sister who has received it directly, but also as "a gift for me." A spirituality of communion means, finally, to know how to "make room" for our brothers and sisters, bearing "each other's burdens" (Gal 6:2) and resisting the selfish temptations which constantly beset us and provoke competition, careerism, distrust and jealousy. (NMI 43)

Necessarily, the spiritual culture of catechists must be markedly communitarian. It should be characterized by the development and promotion of these fraternal attitudes.

The catechist bears "in himself the Church's spirit, her openness to and interest in all peoples and individuals," and in this way "he is a sign of God's love in the world—a love without exclusion or partiality" (RMi 89). In this way, he does not feel like an isolated hero, but rather he feels part of a community. This is only possible if he wants to live it with zeal and ardor, when he looks at the Church with the eyes of Christ and loves her as her spouse loves her, "even to the point of giving one's life" for her (RMi 89). The preacher needs to make of each human group a pure bride to give to Christ (2 Cor 11:2).

This passion for communion leads the catechist to transmit to the catechumens a communitarian style of living the faith and, therefore, a passion for the common good, for justice, for social life. It is true that the catechetical encounter is communitarian by nature. But the love that is learned and practiced in catechesis is called to transcend the limits of the small group.

The gospel that is transmitted in catechesis invites us to commit ourselves to the common good, but not because it is a duty; rather, it is because the catechumen has become passionate about the good of all, especially the poor. The liberating commitment to solidarity and justice should spring from an internal dynamism, from a passionate conviction that spontaneously transforms itself into a way of reacting and acting. The proclamation of the gospel should transmit this social passion to the catechumens, this love that provokes a dedication to the poor, exploited, excluded, weak, and abandoned.

In this case, spirituality is *incarnated* in the depths of the believer, becoming an intense love for the dignity of persons—who are the image of God—and a sincere, vigorous and efficient rejection of everything that means ignoring, hurting, or denigrating that dignity. Only in this way can an integral spirituality be transmitted and developed.

On the other hand, if the Eucharist is the center of catechesis, let us remember that the first thing that the Eucharist produces, from the hearts that receive its grace, is the unity of the brothers and sisters, fraternal communion:

> The Eucharist was instituted so that we might become brothers and sisters; so that from being strangers, scattered and indifferent to one another, we might become one, equal and friends; it is given to us so that from being an apathetic, selfish, divided and hostile mass, we might become a people, a true people, believing and loving with one heart and one soul.[20]

That is why Saint Thomas said that "its effect is the unity of the Mystical Body," because "it is the sacrament of the unity of the Church."[21] Or, in the words of Saint Paul: "Because there is one bread, we who are many are one body, for we all partake of the one bread" (1 Cor 10:17). It must therefore be said that the heart has only truly opened itself to the action of Jesus in the Eucharist when from that heart springs the impulse of fraternal service and the desire to grow in unity. This is possible if the catechist leads to the Eucharist not only his catechumens but also the community of catechists, his brothers and sisters, and the whole community of which he is a part.

But both the lack of generosity and the divisions that can often be seen in communities of catechists show that communion does not produce its effects automatically in each of us, but "according to the measure of our devotion."[22] This cooperation of the loving heart is necessary, which nourishes its devotion but, in addition, also offers itself (Rom 12:1) together with the bread and wine to be an instrument of unity and service:

> In the offering that she presents to God, the Church offers herself.[23]

By offering themselves as an instrument of unity, forgiveness, and mutual service, each catechist will be an instrument of Jesus for the community of catechists to grow in fraternity and generosity, and thus be a luminous sign for the catechumens. Because Jesus said: "[May] they…all be one…so that the world may believe" (John 17:21).

After each Eucharist, a source of unity, each catechist should leave with the firm decision to nourish fraternity with gestures, attitudes, words, encounters, visits, looks, small gifts, and so many other signs that show the authenticity of our love.

That is also spirituality, because it is "spirituality of communion."

Personal Journey

Up to now, our entire spiritual journey has been focused on the catechumens.

But now the time has come to incorporate the other catechists, the rest of the community, and society so that your catechetical spirituality may truly be a "spirituality of communion." For example:

a. Do not stop participating in catechist meetings. In all meetings, try to make them true spiritual spaces, striving to recognize Jesus in the midst of the group, because he is truly there. You must learn to love him not only in solitude or in your work but also in the catechetical community.
b. In those same community meetings, try to treat each catechist as if they were Jesus. It is important that this be expressed in gestures of patience, tenderness, and forgiveness, making others feel valued, respected, and listened to. And also by contributing all the good that you can give with a humble and generous attitude. Everything you do to make each meeting a pleasant and useful moment will be an act of fraternal love and, therefore, a deeply spiritual act that will make you grow in friendship with Jesus.
c. Sometimes you will also have to incorporate your sister and brother catechists into your prayer, praying for them, asking the Lord to give them happiness and fruitfulness, asking for forgiveness for your lack of love toward any of them, asking for the Lord's grace to forgive those who have offended you, giving thanks for their abilities, among other things.
d. But the spirituality of communion, the passion for fraternity, will have to lead you to strengthen ties also with the rest of the community (be it a parish, a school, etc.), collaborating so that the group of catechists

does not isolate itself from the rest. You will have to try to discover what Jesus wants to tell you through the other members of the Christian community. At the same time, if your spirituality is truly fraternal and missionary, you will try to open your heart to the families of your catechumens, the poor in your neighborhood, among others. You will let Jesus awaken your social sensitivity, and you will be concerned about the problems of society. Thus, also, you will be concerned that your catechumens grow in social attitude, so that their hearts open to the problems and sufferings of others. It is essential that this social attitude be an integral part of your spirituality, because the heart does not truly open to God if it is not open to the brothers and sisters.

PASSION FOR GROWTH AND RENEWAL

Catechesis has much to do with the call to grow that God directs to every Christian. In fact, all catechetical activity is at the service of the growth of believers. Therefore, every catechist must be in love with growth.

The catechist is someone who is passionate about God's invitation to develop the life that He gives us. Where a missionary has passed with the first proclamation of the gospel and has begun a journey of conversion, the catechist remains to help grow that new life that has become present.

They are open to growth, not only as a Christian but also as a catechist. This translates into a permanent renewal in his way of understanding the Word, in his methodology, and in his evangelizing ardor.[24] If spirituality is lived in apostolic activity, then the dynamism, which is proper to the life of the Spirit, is also transferred to the activity. This produces a permanent renewal of the task itself. The creativity of the catechist's love is spontaneously transferred to the preparation of a catechesis in constant growth.

Therefore, we can say that a static catechesis, where everything is repeated in the same way year after year, indicates a poverty in spiritual life. It is a spirituality that has stopped growing and, therefore, can no longer promote the necessary apostolic renewal. That catechesis has lost its life, and in this way it has also lost its spiritual depth.

Trust in the action of the Spirit is not merely passive but active and creative. It implies offering oneself as an instrument, with all one's own capacities, so that all those capacities can be used by God: "This evangelizing preaching takes on many forms, and zeal will inspire the reshaping of them almost indefinitely" (EN 43). We see thus how this attitude of trust in the value of the Word implies valuing "the importance of the ways and means" of evangelization (EN 40) and giving oneself over with creative love to the preparation of catechesis.

The Church has, in fact, many ways to reach a large number of people. But to reach them in an effective way, evangelization must always be new in its expression. Only in this way is it possible to effectively reach everyone. That is why catechetical language must be clear, direct, and adapted, but also in a permanent state of change and enrichment, because the world of today, the sensitivity of people, and their language are constantly changing. A living catechesis is always changing. The catechist full of life always tries to "learn to speak according to the mentality and culture of the listeners" (SD 30). He is always learning to be a catechist.

The creative preparation of the encounter implies giving the catechesis an order (Sir 33:4: "prepare what to say"), a structure that makes it comprehensible and interesting (well-presented motivation, development with logic and meaning, clear and timely conclusion), and ensuring that the presentation is brief (Sir 32:8: "Be brief; say much in few words"). It also implies using images (which make what is said pleasant and attractive) and examples (which clarify and concretize it).[25]

Beauty, both in the content and in the accents and in the way of expressing it, is today the best way for the gospel to open a path in hearts. But for that we must always be attentive to discover new ways of expressing ourselves, new tastes, new sensibilities.

It is true that the gospel does not wear out with time and that its message is always valid. But today the world does not accept impositions, and only listens to the message of seduction and testimony. Therefore, the only thing that can allow it to achieve a greater cultural penetration than that of the powerful will be its capacity to re-express itself in the deep interests and in the language of today's man. This applies particularly to spirituality, which is not such if it does not reach the deep inclinations of people. And the human being is always new, society changes permanently, and God himself is always a novelty. A spirituality that does not respond to the new concerns of people cannot penetrate hearts or produce a true transforming dynamism capable of spreading.

The concern for method, even for technique, should be incorporated into this spiritual attitude, which is to respond creatively to the love of God and to love one's neighbor with all one's capacities. And that is also spirituality.

Negligence for the quality of catechesis, and above all the permanent repetition, can indicate a lack of passion for others and for the Word of God. In addition, let us remember that the Creator God wants to prolong himself in the catechist by promoting all his capacities.

He is interested not in a passive, half-dead instrument but rather one that is surrendered and creative. God does not want only our interiority; he wants us whole, using all our mind, our imagination, our sensitivity, all at the service of the mission.

Thus we take up and apply what we said at the beginning of this book: the evangelizing spirituality does not leave out anything that integrates the evangelizing activity. Everything must be placed under the impulse of the Spirit of holiness. Therefore, the responsible path of pastoral planning, preparation, and search for resources and techniques in the light of the Word is also part of this process of sanctification, and it must be lived as a response to the love of God and the impulse of the Spirit. The permanent search for new resources should not be a different or separate reality from the life of the Spirit: it is the life of the Spirit that wants to penetrate and renew everything. A catechesis that has been well prepared in the presence of the Lord, with creativity and dedication, is a true feast of life and hope.

Personal Journey

Now I propose that you make a very particular examination of conscience, with some questions that do not usually appear in examinations of conscience but that you would necessarily have to add to yours, catechist:

a. How has my enthusiasm been for preparing this week's catechetical encounter? What negative things took away my enthusiasm (discouragement, anger, laziness, selfishness, etc.)?
b. Have I tried to give the meeting more order, more clarity, more beauty?
c. Have I tried to find something new in my way of understanding the gospel, in my way of presenting it, in the motivation, in the examples I used, in the activities I proposed in the catechetical encounter?
d. Have I been truly creative or have I simply copied things that others do? Have I put my whole being, my imagination, my creativity, my sensitivity, and all my capacities to renew my catechesis and feel that I am transmitting something that is always new?

Once you have done this examination of conscience, ask the Lord to fill your catechism with life: May he put creativity where there is laziness, put imagination where there is stagnation and repetition. May he put fervor and enthusiasm where there is comfort, that brings newness where something is old and outdated. May he bless all your capacities so that your catechesis may always be growing and in permanent renewal.

CONCLUSION

The Newness of Francis

To close this book, I cannot fail to mention a very important contribution of Pope Francis, which is his invitation to concentrate on the heart of the Christian message, that nucleus we call the *kerygma*. Because returning permanently to the *kerygma* ensures that catechesis does not lose its freshness, its attractiveness, its joy.

When we forget the *kerygma* and are distracted by a lot of data from Christian doctrine, catechesis becomes a paralyzing indoctrination, and the spirituality of the catechist loses its fire, its joy, its color. Because "the biggest problem is when the message we preach then seems identified with those secondary aspects which, important as they are, do not in and of themselves convey the heart of Christ's message" (EG 34).

When a catechist hears the *kerygma* again, "the message has to concentrate on the essentials, on what is most beautiful, most grand, most appealing and at the same time most necessary. The message is simplified, while losing none of its depth and truth, and thus becomes all the more forceful and convincing" (EG 35).

This heart of the gospel "also has a fundamental role in catechesis" because its priority does not mean "it exists at the beginning and can then be forgotten or replaced by other more important things. It is first in a qualitative sense because it is the principal proclamation, the one which we must hear again and again in different ways, the one which we must announce one way or another throughout the process of catechesis, at every level and moment" (EG 164).

This constant return to the amazement of the *kerygma* should not be understood as a loss of doctrinal solidity, because "nothing is more solid, profound, secure, meaningful and wisdom-filled than that initial proclamation" (EG 165). Therefore, the worst risk of catechesis is to have replaced this proclamation with a complex doctrinal instruction, with an obsession with wanting to give thousands of religious information.

Catechesis is a systematic proposal at the service of growth in Christian life, but it seeks above all a greater penetration into this nucleus of the gospel and not so much to add more and more information.

It is interesting to see how Pope Francis applies this to all forms of catechesis, including premarital catechesis:

> They do not need to be taught the entire Catechism or overwhelmed with too much information. Here too, "it is not great knowledge, but rather the ability to feel and relish things interiorly that contents and satisfies the soul." Quality is more important than quantity,

> and priority should be given—along with a renewed proclamation of the *kerygma*—to an attractive and helpful presentation of information that can help couples to live the rest of their lives together "with great courage and generosity." (AL 207)

In this line, it is convenient to assume Francis's insistence on the hierarchy of truths that allows us to concentrate on the great basic themes, four or five flexible axes, renouncing encyclopedism.

The spirituality of the catechist then needs to keep alive the amazement at this proclamation of the *kerygma*, which focuses us on the unconditional love of the Father, the Passover, the personal encounter with Jesus Christ who saves us, and the trust in the action of the Spirit that flows from the heart of Christ. Everything else is secondary and can only be properly understood in the light of this central proclamation.

If a catechist maintains a spirituality full of amazement at this first proclamation, then it will spontaneously spring up in any catechetical encounter, regardless of the topic being dealt with. Thus each topic that is dealt with will contribute something new that allows the *kerygma* to be proclaimed in a different way so that the catechumen may adhere more and more to Jesus, his living redeemer.

We always say that our catechesis will be of little use if we do not manage to get others to live a personal experience of Christ alive who loves and saves them. But it will never be possible to achieve this goal if we ourselves are not deeply focused on this fundamental experience, if we do not recover again and again the experience of being loved and saved.

But this proclamation, Francis teaches, produces an immediate effect on our behavior, which is fraternal love. Then all moral teaching is also simplified and is concentrated on love. Francis puts it explicitly:

> It would not be right to see this call to growth exclusively or primarily in terms of doctrinal formation. It has to do with "observing" all that the Lord has shown us as the way of responding to his love. Along with the virtues, this means above all the new commandment, the first and the greatest of the commandments, and the one that best identifies us as Christ's disciples. (EG 161)

Because "clearly, whenever the New Testament authors want to present the heart of the Christian moral message, they present the essential requirement of love for one's neighbor" (EG 161).

We see that Francis has wanted to "simplify" catechesis and its spirituality in the good sense: that is to say, to concentrate them on the first, on the essential, on the central. And what is essential? It is Christ alive who loves us and saves us and the new commandment of fraternal love. If this is not ignited, burning like fire in our admiring hearts, our catechesis and our spirituality will be only a disordered sum of cold affirmations, without light and without color.

ENDNOTES

1. Cf. J. M. Martínez Beltrán, "Catequista," in *Diccionario abreviado de Pastoral*, ed. C. Floristán and J. J. Tamayo (Estella, 1992), 73–74; E. Alberich, *Catequesis y praxis eclesial* (Madrid, 1983); V. Pedrosa, *La catequesis hoy* (Madrid, 1983).

2. Cf. F. Brossier, *Dire la Bible: Récits bibliques et communication de la foi* (Le Centurion, 1986).

3. Cf. H. U. Von Balthasar, "Palabra y silencio," in *Verbum Caro* (Madrid, 1964), 167–90.

4. Cf. J. Moltmann, *Teología de la esperanza* (Salamanca, 1989).

5. Cf. *Catechism of the Catholic Church*, 1735.

6. Cf. H. Nouwen, D. McNeill, D. Morrison, *Compassion: A Reflection on the Christian Life* (New York, 2005).

7. Cf. C. G. Vallés, *I Love You, I Hate You* (Chicago, 1993).

8. Cf. F. de Vos, *Pensar la catequesis* (Buenos Aires, 1996), 56–63.

9. P. Babin, *La era de la comunicación. Para un nuevo modo de evangelizar* (Santander, 1997), 202.

10. Cf. E. Genre, *Cittadini e discepoli* (Torino, 2000).

11. A. Grün, *El gozo de vivir. Rituales que sanan* (Estella, 1998), 56–57.

12. J. Vanier, *Amar hasta el extremo* (Madrid, 1997), 25.

13. Vanier, *Amar hasta el extremo*, 26.

14. Vanier, *Amar hasta el extremo*, 37.

15. Vanier, *Amar hasta el extremo*, 80–81.

16. Ch. Lubich, "La Eucaristía hace la Iglesia," in *¿Qué significa la Eucaristía para nuestro tiempo?* (Buenos Aires, 1984), 17ss.

17. The base text of the 47th International Eucharistic Congress, "Jesus Christ, the Only Savior of the World: Bread for New Life," 11c.

18. T. Toth, *Eucaristía* (Madrid, 1994), 164.

19. H. J. M. Nouwen, *With Burning Hearts: A Meditation on the Eucharistic Life* (Maryknoll, 2016).

20. Saint Paul VI, in *Insegnamenti di Paolo VI*, Poliglota Vaticana 1966 III, 358.

21. Saint Thomas Aquinas, ST III, 73, 3; IV, 45, 2, 3.

22. Saint Thomas Aquinas ST III, 76, 5.

23. Saint Augustine, *The City of God*, X, 6.

24. Cf. F. van den Bosch, "Situación, experiencia y vida," in *Sociedad de Catequistas Latinoamericanos, Encrucijadas de la Catequesis* (São Paulo, 1999), 56–91. In the same work, cf. L. Alves de Lima, *Traços antropológicos da catequese*, 144–70.

25. Cf. J. Wijngaards, *Communicating the Word of God* (Southend-on-Sea, 1978).